SANT GIANI SUNDER SINGH BHINDRANWALE

ISHWAR SINGH

Made with ♥ on the Notion Press Platform
www.notionpress.com

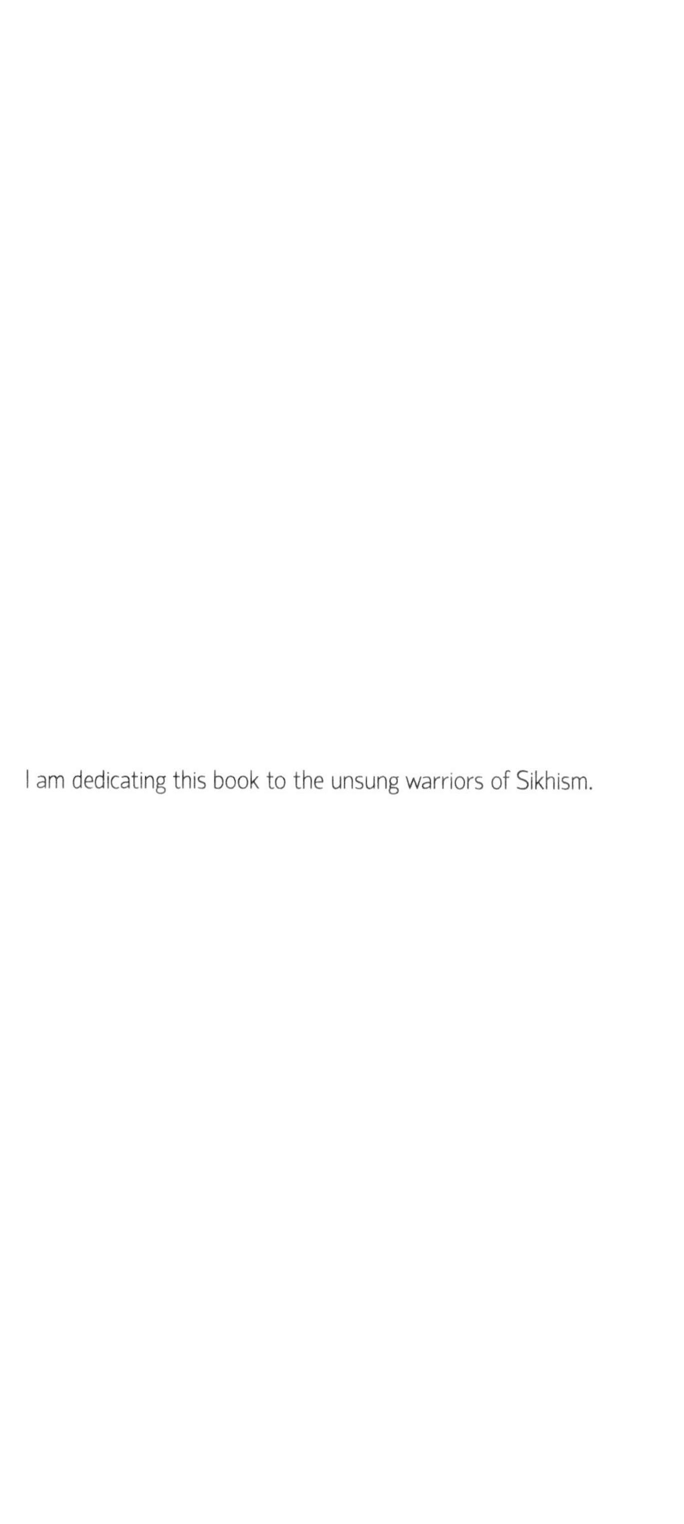

I am dedicating this book to the unsung warriors of Sikhism.

Contents

Foreword

Ishwar Singh have more than ten years of experience in writing story books, sakhis of devotional saints and in research activities. He is a tremendous writer. He is doing excellent job by writing about Sant Giani Sunder Singh Bhindranwale. He had shown very keen interest in the field of religious resources and other cultural issues.

He is also a very excellent teacher and also having deep knowledge about the social science issues. I have always seen him working very hard for his various books. He just want to express about the Indian culture to our new generations in a simple and brief manner. I wish him all the very best for his new book.

Birinder Pal Kaur

Preface

This book is about the brief history of Sant Giani Sunder Singh Bhindranwale. The task behind to publish such content is to spread knowledge about the unsung heroes of the Sikh history among the new generation. In the schools, which are being organised by Sikh trusts, the students are just getting very limited knowledge about the Sikh warriors. Baba Banda Singh Bahadur, Baba Deep Singh etc. are the common names on the tongues of the students but they don't know about the others. This is just an effort to spread this brief information among new generations. I hope that you will like this book.

Acknowledgements

Writing a book is harder than I thought and more rewarding than I could have ever imagined. None of this would have been possible without my best friend, my teacher, my best motivator, my beloved mother Amarjit Kaur. She was the first who inspired me for my goals and taught me various subjects and created my interest specially in Social Sciences. She stood by me during every struggle and all my successes. Whatever I had achieved in my life it is due to my mother.

I'm eternally grateful to my father Pal Singh, who took in an extra mouth to feed when he didn't have to. He taught me discipline, tough love, manners, respect, and so much more that has helped me succeed in life. I truly have no idea where I'd be if he hadn't given me a roof over my head whom I desperately needed at that age.

To my father-in-law Narinder Singh for their moral support during the up and downs in my life. He taught me how to live positive even in the worst situations by sharing his personal experiances. He is the man who suggest me to write a book in your life because it will be your book by which you will be remembered in future.

To Dr. Davinder Singh, who never saw my age, my race, or my lack of formal education. He just saw a kid hungry to learn, hungry to grow, and hungry to succeed in teaching. He never stopped me; he only encouraged me.

Prologue

India is a country of huge cultural diversities. This diversity has its roots in the ancient and medieval period of the history. In present day life, every one is playing his role according to the role assingned by the nature. I have very much interest to explore various great warriors or personalities and cultural aspects of our Indian Society. So an idea came in my mind to explore the brief history of Sant Giani Sunder Singh Bhindranwale. In this book, I have focused on the various achievements of Sant Giani Sunder Singh Bhindranwale. I am writing this book for our younger generations so that when they will read this book, they must understand the sacrifices and struggles of our forefathers.

CHAPTER ONE

Sant Giani Sunder Singh Bhindranwale

In the year 1883, Sri Maan Sant Giani Sundar Singh ji also known as Sant Giani Sundar Singh Muralewale or Sant Giani Sundar Singh Bhindranwale was born in the village of Bhindran Kalan, state of Firozpur, during amrit vela (ambrosial hours, 2AM–5AM). Baba Khajaan Singh was their father, and Bibi Mehtab Kaur was their mother. His parents, who followed the Gursikhi path, assigned him the responsibility of milking the cows and buffaloes when he was between the ages of 6 and 7. This was done in order for them to learn and comprehend Guru Ji's teaching: One who works for what he eats and donates some of what he has. (Sri Guru Granth Sahib, Ang. 1245)

The banis of Panj Granthi, Baaee Vaaraa(n), Bhagat Bani, and Das Granthi were all taught to them simultaneously by their father. When they were between 9 and 10 years old, their father's efforts helped them become Akhand Paathee and taught them how to correctly read Sri Guru Granth Sahib Ji. At this point, they accepted Amrit from Panj Pyare and joined the Khalsa Panth. They lived at home until they were 17 years old, practising their Sikhi practise and studying the essence of Gurbani.

After making an Ardas to Guru Ji for a betterment in their Sikhi and for a greater comprehension of Gurbani, Sant Giani Sundar Singh ji left his house at the age of 18. They arrived at Baba Bishan Singh Ji's sangat in Murale after spending time with a large sangat of Gursikhs and spiritualists. At just two years, they were able to fully comprehend the Gurbani in this place.

They granted Sant Giani Sundar Singh Ji the opportunity to grant them any requests before Sant Bishan Singh Ji ascended to Sach Khand since they had spent their time at Murale performing acts of selflessness. Without any ego, they said, "It is up to you to determine" what you bestow upon me. In order for the sangat to follow the Khalsa path, Sant Bishan Singh Ji proclaimed that they should preach the word of Guru Ji for the remainder of their lives and instruct the sangat in the teachings of Gurbani. They stated that by doing this, Sri Guru Gobind Singh Sahib Ji and Sri Guru Nanak Dev Sahib Ji will always watch over you. Sant Bishan Singh Ji themselves wrapped the dastar of Damdami Taksal around the head of Sant Giani Sundar Singh Ji Bhindranwale on the thirteenth day of the month of Maagh,1905.

To make real the ultimate words of Sant Bishan Singh Ji, they taught the teachings of Guru Ji, consistently going over India. They directed people onto the road of the Khalsa helping them avoid the lies in the world. Sant Giani Sundar Singh Ji would always remember Guru Ji, and everytime they performed Katha, the listeners would experience calmness. By Guru Ji's grace, a miracle took place one day as they were performing a Gurbani Katha: Amrit (nectar) began to leak from a corner of the "chandoaa" (canopy). The Gurdwara sangat became aware of this, and a few even sampled the Amrit and discovered its incredible sweetness.

They taught their pupils that everyone should be proficient in Shastar vidya in addition to being proficient in comprehending Gurbani and always remembering Guru Ji. They would assert that every Sikh ought to be capable of defending and guarding the helpless. They believed it was imperative that every Sikh adhere to Sri Guru Gobind Singh Sahib Ji's directive to be genuine Saint-Soldiers.

They worked hard to promote the five Ks (Kes, Kacchera, Kirpan, Kanga, Kara), saying that they are not just uniforms but rather are meant to advance both our inner and exterior Sikhi practises. The Guru's mandate to wear the 5 Ks is one that many Sikhs have followed, and many more will continue to do so in the future.

Sant Giani Sunder Singh Ji Bhindranwale was giving the Jatha darshan at Sri Darbar Sahib. When they arrived at the location where Baba Deep Singh Ji obtained Shaheed, Sant Ji was doing parkarma. When Sant Ji first turned to look around, the Singhs questioned him as to why they had halted. "Khalsa Ji, there will be a Damdami Taksal's Jathedar that will come here, and when he comes, the Indian government will strike here with their army," Sant Ji said in response to the question of why they were staring about.

After the incident, the Damdami Taksal Jathedar will flee; many will believe he has attained shaheed, but only one person will be aware of his whereabouts and expected return date. Sant Ji added that when he makes a reappearance, he would return from the Atari Border with fauj as a jang is taking place. He will arrive at Sri Darbar Sahib immediately away to listen to kirtan before engaging in combat in the jang to secure Khalsa Rule for the Sikh nation.

A sevadar for the Jatha from the time of Sant Giani Sunder Singh Ji Bhindranwale until the time of Sant Baba Thakur Singh Ji Khalsa, Bibi Daleep Kaur Boparai Wali, who was 13 at the time, was present when this bachan from Sant Giani Sunder Singh Ji Bhindranwale occurred in front of the jatha at that time. A few years ago, she departed for Sachkhand Sahib.

Sant Ji converted 10,000 individuals to Amtidhari Sikhs at once in the English Raaj. After they had taken Amrit, Sant Ji gathered all the Singhs and Singhnians together. The men sent them to the Jaito Morcha for shaheedi while the women wore black chunees. The English then ordered S.S.P. Nanak Singh to go after Sant Giani Sunder Singh Ji Bhindranwale, but Nanak Singh refused, claiming that Sant Ji is a very strong Sikh and that if he did, they would destroy their Raaj. Because they didn't want to jeopardise their Raaj, the English were just not ready to go and capture Sant Ji at that time.

Sant Giani Sundar Singh Ji was quite unwell due to a chronic ailment in 1929 AD, yet he always had a positive outlook on life. They consistently kept Guru Ji at the centre of their attention. One of their pupils, Giani Gurbachan Singh Ji Khalsa, received the selfless service of carrying on Sri Guru Gobind Singh Ji's Damdami Taksal from them.

On February 15, 1930 (AD), at around 8:15 AM, in the village of Boparai at Gurdwara Sachkhand, they departed the soil for the charan of Guru Sahib at the instruction of Guru Ji.

They finished Sri Guru Granth Sahib Ji's Katha 21 times during their lifetime. They had roughly 1300 students when they finished their service, of whom 1000 became Akhand Paathees, 200 became preachers, and 100 became katha vaachiks. Sant ji covered all of the expenses that their pupils spent. Sant Giani Sundar Singh Ji dedicated their entire life to serving the Khalsa Panth in a selfless manner.

Sant Giani Sunder Singh Bhindranwale